Forgiven
490

Donald Peart

Forgiven 490 © 2011 Donald Peart.

Cover design by Jeshua Peart

ISBN: 978-0-9852481-6-1

Printed in the United States of America

All "bold" emphasis in the references is supplied by the author.
All literal parenthetical phrases in the Scripture references are added by the author.

Dictionary reference, includes, but not limited to, Strong's Concordance, BibleWorks Software, and ISA2 Basic Software

Edition: September 2022

Acknowledgment

It seemed good to our Father, the Father of our Lord Jesus Christ, who desired to have these things written. Thanks to you Father for your forgiveness of our sins.

Thanks to Judith, the wife of my youth and our children (Donald Jr., Jeshua, Charity, Benjamin, and Jesse) for allowing me the time to continue to write. They are indeed in Christ Jesus and forgiven through the blood of Jesus Christ.

Thanks to a Church of our Lord Jesus Christ (Crown of Glory Ministries) who we currently oversee, and who are also forgiven through the blood of Jesus Christ.

Table of Contents

Introduction 1
Jesus Anointed to Forgive! 2
The Ministry of Reconciliation... 5
Forgiveness of Every Sin.. 9
"There is a Sin unto Death" 12
How to Receive Forgiveness 17
Seventy Times Seven Forgiveness.. 21
"Seventy Sevens" to End Sins 23
490 Forgiveness in Every Measure... 27
The Bosom of 490 Forgiveness 30
How often do we forgive? 32
Forgiven Ten Thousand Times 35
No More Consciousness of Sins.. 38
The Examples of Forgiveness.. 41
There is no Condemnation 44

Introduction

"Forgiven, 490 Times" was written because of the broad need of Jesus' disciples and the unbelieving to understand what forgiveness really means, and the tangible relief experienced in one's conscience through the forgiveness of sins. There are some in the world (those outside of the Church) who do not even believe that they need to be forgiven of any sins. I hope this book also bring those kinds of thinkers to the knowledge of our Lord Jesus Christ, and the forgiveness of sins that He has afforded to all mankind. There are also those who go through life without closure to guilt.

To know one is forgiven of guilt, or to know that one is forgiven for an offense can bring closure to inner wounds. The Spirit of Jesus is here to make you whole! I have not met anyone who does not like "debt relief." This is what Jesus also does for us, He "releases"[1] (forgives) our debts (sins); and He does not remember them. We will see in this book that Jesus is very compassionate towards those who ask for His mercy and forgiveness. I have not read in the Scriptures where Jesus denied anyone who asked Him for forgiveness.

So, I expect that this book about Jesus and His forgiveness will be of relief to you, and that you in turn may be able to comfort others!

---

[1] The Greek compound word (apohiemi) translated as "forgiveness" or "forgive," literally means "from-send" (to send from) or "to release."

Jesus Anointed to Forgive!

Luke 4:18, NKJ

*The Spirit of the LORD is upon Me because He has **anointed** Me to preach the gospel to the poor; He has sent Me to heal the brokenhearted, to proclaim **liberty** to the captives and recovery of sight to the blind, to **set at liberty** those who are oppressed.*

Jesus was and is anointed to forgive. The verse above reads in the Greek as such: "The Spirit of the Lord is upon Me, because He **anointed** Me ... to proclaim **'forgiveness'** to the **captives,** and ... to 'send in **forgiveness'** them that are 'shattered to minute particles'."

Jesus, in one of His first declarations, indicated that the "captives" need to be "forgiven" and those whose lives are "shattered" also need to be "forgiven." The forgiveness of Jesus flows from the **anointing** of the Holy Spirit. "The Spirit of the Lord ... has **anointed Me** to ... proclaim forgiveness and ... to 'commission' in forgiveness ...."

There are many who claim to have the anointing of the Lord Jesus yet cannot forgive! The Scripture states that it is Satan who does not forgive. Thus, it is satanic not to forgive those who repent of their offenses *(Luke 17:3).*

2 Corinthians 2:10-11, NKJ

[10] *Now whom you **forgive** anything, I also forgive. For if indeed I have **forgiven** anything, I have **forgiven** that one for your sakes in the presence of Christ,* [11]*lest Satan should **take advantage (lit., that no larger portion)** of us; for we are not ignorant of his devices (lit., thoughts).*

The Scripture states that Satan gets the "advantage," or literally, "a larger part," "to overreach," "to have more" of any, if one refuses to forgive. Any thought of not wanting to forgive is a satanic "thought." In contrast, the "thoughts" of God are "higher" than Satan and mankind. God's thoughts are thoughts of "mercy and they "abundantly pardon."

Isaiah 55:7-9, NKJ
*⁷Let the wicked forsake his way, And the unrighteous man his **thoughts**; Let him return to the LORD, And He will have mercy on him; And to our God, For He will abundantly **pardon (lit. forgive)**. ⁸"For My **thoughts are not your thoughts**, nor are your ways My ways," says the LORD. ⁹"For as the heavens are higher than the earth, so are My ways higher than your ways, And **My thoughts than your thoughts**."*

"The unrighteous man" must "forsake ... **his thoughts;** and return ... to our God, and He **(God) will have mercy** ... He **(God) will abundantly forgive." For** My (God's) thoughts are not your (ours) thoughts." The conjunction **"for"** in the reference above connects the two verses. Therefore, God's thoughts are mercy and abundance of forgiveness. The true anointing forgives! The anointing from the Holy One is also an anointing to forgive. There is "release" in forgiveness! Shattered lives can be put together again by forgiveness!

Dr Kelley Varner, who mentored me for nearly fifteen years, and became as a father to me four years before his passing, recounted an event that occurred on his way back home from a ministry trip abroad. He said, as the airplane landed, he heard the voice of the Lord say to him, **"I am going to deliver my creation through forgiveness."**

This is the heart of the Father; He has granted His creation the forgiveness of sins through the blood of Jesus *(Colossians 1:14)!* **"All"** have sinned" *(see Romans 3:23).* Therefore "all" are candidates to be forgiven by the Lord Jesus.

There are so many who are so self-condemned and some who are condemned by others, and therefore feel that they are unforgivable. I am here to tell you that belief is not true! Jesus, the Christ was anointed to forgive us of all types of sins with one exception. Jesus is not like mankind whose hearts are hard to forgive. Jesus is Mercy. In fact, Jesus so loved, He took the punishment we deserved for our sins, so that we would not have to be punished eternally, as long as we accept Jesus' salvation.

Jesus' death on the cross was an "exchange" for us. He died so we do not have to die eternally for our sins. He was punished for our sins on the cross so we may be forgiven from going to the lake of fire and lightning. Jesus was also raised from the dead to enforce our release from the captivity of sins. Here is a fact! **You will be forgiven by the Lord Jesus if you ask Him for His mercy, accepting Jesus' blood that was shed for you.**

I have not found anywhere in the New Testament where Jesus denied someone's request for His mercy. This same living Jesus will forgive you now! All you have to do is **ask** Him from your heart, and then **"trust"** Him that He has forgiven you. Jesus was anointed to forgive. He is still anointed to forgive YOU! "God was in **'the Anointed One'** reconciling the world unto Himself not **'taking inventory'** of their trespasses" *(2 Corinthians 5:19).*

The Ministry of Reconciliation

The Spirit of Jesus laid it on my wife Judith's heart to share a message on "The Ministry of Reconciliation" at a Wednesday night Bible study. I thought it appropriate to honor her by sharing her beautiful lesson at this point in the book. Here is Judith:

> As ministers (or believers) we have a responsibility to reconcile the world back to God through Christ. Paul says in *2 Corinthians 5:11* that because we know the **terror** of the Lord, we **persuade** men. But how do we **persuade** men as ministers and believers? First, we must see that word "persuade," indicates that we "persuade" others by winning them; we persuade others by stirring them with God's words to believe; or we convince them to have faith in a Person—Jesus.
>
> The ministry of reconciliation and its main purpose, according to *2 Corinthians 5:17,* is to make everyone in Christ a "new creation," where "old things are passed away," and all things have become "new." God wants to save "all" and bring them to Christ, no matter how they see themselves or what they may feel they have done. The word "new" is a Greek word which means new in form and quality, fresh, unused, novel, a new kind.
>
> As God reconciles you back to Himself through Jesus; He is turning you into a whole new person inside and out. He is accepting anyone who wants to come to Him and to change their hearts and way of life; and He is giving them a "new form."
>
> This "new form" is a new pattern—the life of Jesus. The Bible says be imitators of God as dear children and walk in love. The word "imitator" is compared to a child who

traces a letter in handwriting because the pattern has already been made for the child to follow the tracings. When Jesus makes us a new creature, we must follow His form and become like Him. In doing so, we teach others to be like Him as well.

In *2 Corinthians 5:17,* I like the idea that the old things, the sinful nature, is dead when we turn to Christ, and a whole "new kind" of person emerges from the dust of the "old man." God, the potter, then forms or makes us. This new person is a person that you and the world have yet to see.

You will develop inside in a way that you have never known. When sin dominates our lives and the lives of the unsaved, we smother the real purposes and gifts within us. The gifts, character, and love that were placed in us become tainted if sin rules. When Christ comes, we learn for the first time why we were created and what we were created to do.

So, in essence we are made new, restored. We feel unused and fresh again for the first time in our lives. *John 3:3* calls this the "new birth;" and "except a man be **born again** he cannot see the kingdom of God."

According to *2 Corinthians 5:18,* God has reconciled us to Himself through Jesus Christ! He has given us the ministry of reconciliation. Reconciliation is a Greek word which means "change or exchange." It is also defined as Jesus' "atonement." With a little play on the word "atonement," one can see "at-one-ment." **That is, Jesus makes us and others one with God again.** Jesus was the substitute for us.

He was the Lamb of God that took away our sin on the cross. We should have been judged instantly for our sins, but God exchanged Jesus for us. We know man is a falling creature, because of the sins of Adam and Eve passed upon all men *(see Romans 5: 12).*

We who are saved from death, have a responsibility to offer this "service or ministry of reconciliation" to those who are lost and cannot find their way to God.

The **"Ministry of Reconciliation,"** through Jesus Christ, is a tool for spreading the good news of Jesus and the kingdom of God. By proclaiming and promoting the gospel of God concerning Jesus Christ and His "exchange" (He being the sacrifice for all mankind), we let mankind know that there is an exchange for their sins. He (Jesus) is the exchange. He took our sin and punishment and gave us his life. Glory to God!

According to *2 Corinthians 5:11,* God gave us the ministry of reconciliation! We spread this word by telling the world that God is working in Jesus to bring them back to God, the Father, by **not imputing** our trespasses to us!

The word "imputing" means to keep inventory or record of your sins. When you accepted or accept Jesus as your savior, God no longer keeps inventory of your sins. There is no more record of what you have done or what was done to you. It is the ministry of forgiveness.

God has released your sins and forgiven you, and now we as believers have a responsibility to offer this service Jesus is offering to others. He wants to reconcile all back to God without imputing or keeping records of their wrongdoing. The blood of Jesus is strong enough to wash away not just sins but the consciousness of sin—the memories that keep people awake at night and torment them from day to day.

Only Jesus can destroy the defilement and soil of sin, and the deathly effects it has on mankind. Now we all have a ministry, a service, in God to bring people back to God. He has exchanged our sins by giving us His righteousness; and He is the atonement (the one who has covered our sins forever).

In conclusion, now that we as believers have received this atonement and exchange, we are ambassadors for Christ. We are sent by Him to tell others that they too can be reconciled back to God, no matter what sins they have committed (except blasphemy of the Holy Spirit which is calling the spirit of God evil). Remember you have the word of reconciliation. Win and persuade men, by the terror or by the fear you have of God by telling them to be reconciled to God through Jesus the Christ.

To the unsaved and to the backslider, I say: as Paul said, "As though God were pleading through us: we implore *you* on Christ's behalf, be reconciled to God" *(2 Corinthians 5:20, NKJ).*

By Judith Peart

Forgiveness of Every Sin

Matthew 12:31, NKJ
*Therefore, I say to you, **every sin and blasphemy will be forgiven men,** but the blasphemy against the Spirit will not be forgiven men.*

Mark 3:28, NKJ
*Assuredly, I say to you, **all sins will be forgiven the sons of men,** and whatever blasphemies they may utter.*

Jesus said, "All sins will be forgiven" mankind except for the sin that causes one "not to [be able to] hold forgiveness...." I repeat; there are not any sins the Father will not forgive humans for, except for one sin. If a person sins in this life, with any sins, except one, and that person asks the Father for forgiveness through Jesus Christ, the Father will grant forgiveness! (The only sin that the Father will not forgive is "blasphemy against the Spirit;" and we will discuss later, this sin that carries over into the age to come.

We are blessed to be forgiven through Jesus for every other sin we may commit. "Just as David also describes the blessedness of the man to whom God imputes righteousness apart from works: Blessed are those whose lawless deeds are forgiven, and whose sins are covered; blessed is the man to whom the LORD shall not impute sin." *(Romans 4:6-8, NKJ).*

"The Lord will not **reckon** sin" to those who ask for forgiveness through Jesus Christ! "Reckon" in the Greek literally means "to take an inventory." This is the love of our Father, the Father of the Lord Jesus Christ. Once we ask the Father for forgiveness, He does not keep any "inventory" of our sins in this age or the ages to come; and we are "pronounced" "blessed" because of the Father's forgiveness. The Father "**imputes** to us righteousness apart from works." We do not have to work to receive His righteousness. He forgives us and reckons to us His righteousness; and the Father, the Lord Jesus and the Holy Spirit do not keep inventory of any sins; we are forgiven.

Hebrews 10:16-18, NKJ
[16]*"This is the covenant that I will make with them after those days, says the LORD: I will put My laws into their hearts, and in their minds, I will write them,"* [17]*then He adds,* **"Their sins and their lawless deeds I will remember no more."** [18]*Now where there is remission of these, there is no longer an offering for sin.*

What a consoling statement. Once the Father forgives our sins and iniquities, the Father does not "remember" our sins and iniquities. The Father does not keep inventory of our sins and lawless deeds, once we ask for forgiveness. The Father is not like humans!

We tend to remember our sins and the sins of others all the days we live. We must change that mindset. We must become like the Father; we must forgive and forget any offenses. This is the kindness of God that was personified in Jesus.

Titus 3:4-6, NKJ
[4]*But when the* **kindness** *and the* **love** *of God our Savior toward man appeared,* [5]*not by works of righteousness which we have done, but according to His mercy He saved us, through the washing of regeneration and renewing of the Holy Spirit,* [6]*whom He poured out on us abundantly through Jesus Christ our Savior.*

Jesus is the kindness of God; and "according to His mercy He saved us." "Not by works of righteousness which we have done." The Father forgives our sins without any work we may do. The Father forgives our sins and does not remember them anymore. The Father forgives our sins and does not keep or take any inventory of sins He has forgiven us for. What a relief! This is the wonderful grace of God. Paul said that the Father's love is so high, so broad, so deep, and so long towards us, that it surpasses our understanding. Our brains cannot fathom that our Father in heaven loves us so much that He does not keep inventory of our sins; neither does He remember them after he forgives us.

He appears to "abundantly" set "precedence" in the area of forgiveness. He has the right to precede others in forgiveness. He will forgive you of all your sins before others may! The Father, the Lord Jesus and the Holy Spirit are to be feared because there is forgiveness with them!

Psalm 130:3-4; 7-8, ASV
*³ **If** you, O LORD, kept a **record** of sins, O Lord, who could stand? ⁴But with you there is **forgiveness;** therefore, you are **feared** ... ⁷ O Israel, put your hope in the LORD, for with the LORD is unfailing love and with him is **full redemption (or, "abundance of precedence").** ⁸He himself will redeem Israel from **all their sins.***

"There is a Sin unto Death"

1 John 5:16, NKJ
*If anyone sees his brother sinning a sin which does not lead to death, he will ask, and He will give him life for those who commit sin not leading to death. **There is sin leading to death.** I do not say that he should pray about that.*

Jesus forgives all sins, except for one sin, the sin of blasphemy against the Spirit. This is the sin that John, the beloved of Jesus, was referring to in the verse above. He called this sin "a sin leading to death." This sin unto **death** appears to be the sin of blasphemy. This "death" I believe is the "second death" – the lake of fire and brimstones.

Before I speak of this sin of blasphemy, I must say that anyone who has the Spirit of God cannot blaspheme the Holy Spirit. The Holy Spirit cannot speak against himself. The Holy Spirit is translated literally as the "Clean Spirit." He cannot ever be defiled; and those who really have the "Clean Spirit" in them cannot speak evil of the "Clean Spirit."

1 Corinthians 12:3, NIV
*Therefore, I tell you that **no one who is speaking by the Spirit of God says, "Jesus be cursed,"** and no one can say, "Jesus is Lord," except by the Holy Spirit.*

Blasphemy against the Spirit is "a sin unto death." It is a sin that carries over into the eternal age. This sin will not be forgiven "into the age." Forgiveness of sins through the blood of Jesus is effective to blot out sins in this life and also in eternity. The effectiveness of forgiveness is that forgiveness is permanent in eternity, even though some sins that are forgiven may have repercussions in this life, because of the laws of the land.[2] However, the sin of blasphemy against the Holy Spirit is not forgiven in this age or the age to come.

Matthew 12:31, NKJ
*Therefore, I say to you, every sin and blasphemy will be forgiven men, **but the blasphemy against the Spirit will not be forgiven men.***

Mark 3:29, NKJ
*But he who blasphemes against the Holy Spirit never has forgiveness but is subject to **eternal condemnation.***

Matthew was pretty assertive. Blasphemy of the Holy Spirit "shall not be forgiven." That person is subject to "eternal judgment." **According to Mark's gospel, that person "who blasphemes against the Holy Spirit is not holding forgiveness but is holding-in eternal judgment."** The question is: how does Jesus defines blasphemy? Blasphemy is to say that the "Holy (lit., Clean) Spirit" is an unclean spirit. Blasphemy unto death is to say that Jesus was/is performing His miraculous work through an unclean spirit.

Mark 3:29-30, NKJ
*[29]But he who **blasphemes against the Holy Spirit never** has forgiveness, but is subject to eternal condemnation [30]because they said, "He has an unclean spirit."*

The verse above declares the unpardonable sin. The unpardonable sin is to say that the Holy Spirit is an unclean spirit. The Pharisees and teachers of the law claimed that Jesus was casting out demons by Beelzebub, the prince of devils. This, friend, is blasphemy, to say that Jesus cast out demons with an unclean spirit—and not just any unclean spirit—but to accuse Jesus of doing His work through Beelzebub? Let us read Mark

---

[2] A statement made by David Dayton of Newport News, VA

and Matthew's accounts of those who committed the sin unto death—blasphemy against the Holy Spirit.

Mark 3:22; 28-30, NKJ

22And the scribes who came down from Jerusalem said, "He has Beelzebub," and, "By the ruler of the demons He casts out demons …. 28"Assuredly, I say to you, all sins will be forgiven the sons of men, and whatever blasphemies they may utter; 29"but he who blasphemes against the Holy Spirit never has forgiveness but is subject to eternal condemnation" – 30 because they said, "He has an unclean spirit."

Matthew 12:22-25; 31-32, ASV

22 Then they brought him a demon-possessed man who was blind and mute, and Jesus healed him, so that he could both talk and see. 23 All the people were astonished and said, "Could this be the Son of David?" 24But when the Pharisees heard this, they said, "It is only by Beelzebub, the prince of demons, that this fellow drives out demons." 25 Jesus knew their thoughts and said to them …. 31 … I tell you, every sin and blasphemy will be forgiven men, but the blasphemy against the Spirit will not be forgiven. 32 Anyone who speaks a word against the Son of Man will be forgiven, but anyone who speaks against the Holy Spirit will not be forgiven, either in this age or in the age to come.

The fact that this sin "will not be forgiven in this age or the age to come" makes it a sin that is carried over into eternity. Every sin and lawlessness that is forgiven by God is forgotten by the Father; or covered by Him through the blood of Jesus into eternity. However, the sin of blasphemy against the Spirit of God has eternal effects. It is carried over to "the age to come" and those who are liable of the eternal judgment will be affected by the second death—the lake of fire. "There is a sin that leads to death. I am not saying that he should pray about that" *(1 John 5:16c, NIV).*

Remember, Jesus said "Every sin and blasphemy shall be forgiven unto men." Thus, you should not panic if you have blasphemed in some areas. The great apostle Paul blasphemed, and Jesus forgave him *(1 Timothy 1:13).* Thus, every blasphemy is forgiven men, except blasphemy against the Holy Spirit.

For a person to blaspheme the Holy Spirit, that person has to have the fullness of blasphemy in his or her mind or heart. This full-fledged blasphemy in the mind of man is linked to the "name of the beast" (which is blasphemy); or "the mark of [the beast's] name" (the character of blasphemy); or the "number of [the beast] name" (666 — man's evil words against the Holy Spirit).

Revelation 13:1, ASV
*And he stood upon the sand of the sea. And I saw **a beast** coming up out of the sea ... and upon his heads **names of blasphemy.***

Revelation 13:17, NKJ
*And that no one may buy or sell except one who has the mark or the **name of the beast,** or the **number of his name.***

Revelation 14:11, NKJ
*And ... they have no rest day or night ... whoever receives **the mark of his name.***

Revelation 13:5-6, NKJ
*[5]And **he** was given a mouth speaking great things and **blasphemies,** and he was given authority to continue for forty-two months. [6]Then he opened his mouth in **blasphemy** against God, to blaspheme His **name,** His **tabernacle,** and **those who dwell in heaven.***

The beast's name is blasphemy. Thus, the beast is true to its name, as were the Pharisees and some of blasphemous teachers of the law who blasphemed Jesus and His Holy Spirit. The beast blasphemed God, God's name, God's tabernacle (His Church) and even "those" (angels, men, and other creature) who dwell in heaven.

However, if a person has the "Clean Spirit" and thus he or she is speaking in the Holy Spirit, he/she cannot blaspheme the Spirit of Jesus. Thus, if you have the Holy Spirit (the Spirit of Promise); any sins, blasphemies, and lawlessness is forgiven you through the blood of Jesus once you ask Him for forgiveness. So be it! May the Father be thanked and may the name of Jesus be blessed for ever more!

1 John 1:8-10, NKJ
8If we say that we have no sin, we deceive ourselves, and the truth is not in us. 9If we confess our sins; He is faithful and just to forgive us our sins and to cleanse us from all unrighteousness. 10If we say that we have not sinned, we make Him a liar, and His word is not in us.

How to Receive Forgiveness

Matthew 6:12-14, NKJ
12And forgive us our debts, as we forgive our debtors. 13And do not lead us into temptation but deliver us from the evil one. For Yours is the kingdom and the power and the glory forever. Amen. ***14For if you forgive men their trespasses, your heavenly Father will also forgive you.***

Luke 11:4, NKJ
*And forgive us our sins, for we also forgive everyone who is indebted to us. And **do not lead us into temptation but** deliver us from the evil one.*

Jesus said that when we ask for forgiveness, we receive forgiveness because we have forgiven others who were indebted to us. The Lord Jesus said, "Forgive us our sins, **for we also** forgive everyone who is indebted to us." That is, if we can find it in our hearts to forgive others who have sinned against us, then our heavenly Father will forgive us in the same manner.

There is also another truth. The same speed by which you forgive others is the same speed by which the Father forgives our sins. There is a temptation not to forgive people of their offenses speedily; thus, Jesus' statement immediately after His directive to forgive. Listen to Jesus' statement in Luke: "And forgive us our sins, **for** we also forgive everyone who is indebted to us. And **do not lead us into temptation.**" The "temptation" of not being willing to forgive!

In other words, if we find it hard to ask the Father for forgiveness, and we find it hard to believe He has forgiven us, it is probably because we have not forgiven someone who has sinned against us. Let us avoid the temptation not to forgive. Jesus' encouragement guides us to always forgive others. Why? We want to be forgiven always for all things by God, the Father.

We must love our neighbors **as** we love ourselves. The opposite is also true. We can only show love to others to the degree we love ourselves. In other words, we find it difficult to forgive others because we do not love ourselves. If we do not love ourselves, we find it difficult to receive forgiveness from God.

Galatians 5:14, NKJ
*… You shall love your neighbor **as** yourself.*

With that said, we must also believe that we are forgivable! An epidemic among mankind is that some people do not believe that they are forgivable. In fact, some increase sinning in their lives because they believe there is no hope for them. I believe that one of the reasons why the Pharisees were calloused enough to do the unpardonable sin is because they were "not holding (accepting) forgiveness." Concerning the Pharisees, Jesus said to them: "He who blasphemes against the Holy Spirit is **'not holding forgiveness,'** but is **'holding-in** eternal 'verdict'" (*Mark 3:29, as it reads literally (refer to interlinear translations).*

We know for sure that they also did not forgive the sins of others **(Luke 7:39, John 9:34, John 8:3-5).** Instead, they were "holding-in eternal 'verdicts,'" especially against others. Thus, according to the apostle Paul, the Pharisees must have not loved themselves. One of the keys to receiving forgiveness is to love **you** in a healthy manner! Believe that **you** are forgivable!

Ephesians 5:29a, NKJ
For no one ever hated his own flesh ….

One of the ways to receive forgiveness is to know that God loves you. You must also love yourself. There are some that hate their own flesh. Some hate themselves because they have received no love from natural parents, family, friends, etc. Thus, some believe they are unforgivable!

Some also hate themselves so much because of their past mistakes. They think that the Father will not forgive them. However, through Jesus Christ, "All of man's sins will be forgiven." Paul said man is not supposed to hate his own flesh. We must love ourselves, so that we can love our neighbors. If we hate ourselves, we make it difficult for ourselves to receive forgiveness.

We must know we are forgivable in order to forgive our neighbor. If we hate ourselves, we will hate others. If we love our selves, we will love others. We must receive the forgiveness of the Father by loving ourselves— **"no one ever hated his own flesh."**

Finally, I believe more importantly, we receive forgiveness by **trust.** Jesus Christ is the end of animal sacrifices to receive forgiveness. We must now **trust in Jesus,** in the sacrifice of Jesus Christ for the forgiveness of sins. "For Christ is the end of the law for righteousness to everyone who **believes (lit., trusts)"** *(Romans 10:4, NKJ).*

Hebrews 10:4, NKJ
For it is not possible that the blood of bulls and goats could take away sins.

Hebrews 10:10, NKJ
*By that will we have been sanctified through the offering of the body of Jesus Christ **once for all.***

It is not possible for the blood of bulls and goats to take away our sins. However, it is a blessed truth, "we have been sanctified through the offering of the body of Jesus Christ **once for all.**" Thus, we do not need any animal sacrifices ever again.

With that said, it is by **trust** in His blood that we are redeemed. We have to **trust** the Father that He has forgiven us through the blood of Jesus Christ. We only please God by **trust** (a definition for **faith**) *(Hebrews 11:6).*

Romans 3:23-27, NKJ
*23 for all have sinned and fall short of the glory of God, 24 being justified freely by His grace through the redemption that is in Christ Jesus, 25 whom God set forth as a propitiation by His blood, through **faith,** to demonstrate His righteousness, because in His forbearance God had **passed over** the sins that were previously committed, 26to demonstrate at the present time His righteousness, that He might be just and the justifier of the one who has faith **(or, trusts)** in Jesus. 27Where is boasting then? It is excluded. By what law? Of works? No, but by the law of faith (lit., law of trust).*

Thus, we see that we receive forgiveness by trust in Jesus' sacrifice of Himself for us. We are not to trust not in our own good works for salvation. "For by grace you have been **saved through faith,** and that not of yourselves; it is the gift of God," *(Ephesians 2:8, NKJ).*

We also receive forgiveness by loving ourselves. If we hate our selves, it will be difficult to believe that the Father forgive us. This flows over into the other way to receive forgiveness. If we forgive (love) our neighbors, we can also receive forgiveness from the heavenly Father as we forgive others.

Seventy Times Seven Forgiveness

Matthew 18:21-22, NKJ
[21]*Then Peter came to Him and said, "Lord, how often shall my brother sin against me, and I forgive him? Up to seven times?"* [22]*Jesus said to him, "I do not say to you, up to seven times, but up to **seventy times seven.**"*

Luke 17:3-4, NKJ
[3]*"Take heed to yourselves. If your brother sins against you, rebuke him; and if he repents, forgive him.* [4]*And if he sins against you seven times in a day, and seven times **in a day** returns to you, saying, 'I repent,' you shall forgive him."*

Jesus said the number of forgiveness is seventy times seven. That is, four hundred and ninety times a day we are to forgive each other. Peter asked Jesus, how many times are we to forgive a person for sinning against us, seven times? Jesus responded to Peter, by saying, "Until seventy times seven." Jesus, through Luke's Gospel gave more detail by saying "seven times **in a day.**" Thus, the seventy times seven also applies to each day.

That is a lot of forgiveness in one day. I believe being forgiven four hundred-ninety times a day is practically inexhaustible. A person would have to sin approximately once every three minutes per day to sin four hundred-ninety times in one day! Who would willingly tempt God with such acts?

If Jesus requires us to forgive others four hundred-ninety (490) times in a day, then the Father does the same for us. God does not ask us to do something He Himself would not do. Years ago, while in engineering school, I worked at a Jewish nursing home. I met a Jew named Benjamin. During one of our conversations, he told me that if a Jewish father disciplines his son or daughter not to have ice cream for an evening, the father of the household will also do the same. The same principle is true for our heavenly Father. The Father will not ask us to do something that He is not willing to do Himself.

The heavenly Father said we are to ask the Father to "forgive us our debts, **as** we also have forgiven our debtors" *(Matthew 6:12).* When we forgive our debtors four hundred-ninety (490) times, the Father will also forgive our debts, four hundred-ninety (490) times. The ways of the Lord are equal or balanced.

Being forgiven four hundred-ninety (490) times in a day is a beautiful truth. God does not get impatient with us, as we are not to run out of forgiveness for our fellow brothers and sisters. In fact, 490 is the number of forgiveness that ends sin. In other words, the more the heavenly Father forgives us, the less we sin. Condemnation does not end or prevent sins. Jesus' forgiveness delivers us from sins. As indicated earlier, Dr Varner said that the Lord told him that He (God) would "deliver his creation through forgiveness!"

"Seventy Sevens" to End Sins

Daniel 9:24, NKJ
Seventy weeks (lit., seventy sevens) are determined for your people and for your holy city, to finish the transgression, to make an end of sins, to make reconciliation for iniquity, to bring in everlasting righteousness, to seal up vision and prophecy, and to anoint the Most Holy.

When Jesus used the phrase seventy times seven in Matthew 18, it was a deliberate statement with prophetic overtone in regard to His life.

Gabriel, one of the arch angels used the same terms with respect to Jesus in Daniel 9:24-27. We learn in Daniel that seventy sevens relates to ending sins with the view to bringing in everlasting righteousness, etc.

As indicated before, forgiveness of sins ends sins! Condemnation for sins perpetuates sins. Think of it! Condemnation of oneself for sins or condemnation by others usually perpetuates guilt. There is a remembrance of sins being made through "down-judging."

However, when our heavenly Father forgives us of a particular sin, that sin is no longer remembered by Him. Thus, that sin is ended. When the heavenly Father does **not keep inventory** of our sins, those sins are ended.

They are not found in any **inventory.** If we sin four hundred-ninety times in a day, the Lord will forgive us. Why? He wants to end sins. This is the principle outlined in Daniel's famous prophesy given to him by the mouth of Gabriel.

There are six (6) things that are to occur during the seventy weeks (lit., seventy sevens) prophesied by Daniel concerning Jesus.

Here are the "six" things that pertain to "man" during the "seventy sevens," or 490 years.

Seventy sevens are decreed:

1. To finish transgression
2. To make an end of sins (or sin offerings)
3. To make reconciliation for iniquity
4. To bring in everlasting righteousness
5. To seal up the Vision (Jesus) and prophecy (Jesus)
6. To anoint the Most Holy (Jesus, the Church, and the heavenly things)

It follows, when Jesus asks us to forgive others seventy times seventy, forgiveness is linked to the ending of un-forgiveness and the bringing in of Jesus' reconciliation and righteousness, as we see in items 2, 3 and 4 above.

1. Jesus' "490 forgiveness" "restricts" or "holds back" our transgressions.

Romans 4:15, NKJ
*Because the law brings about wrath; **for where there is no law there is no transgression.***

Hebrews 9:15, NKJ
*And for this reason, He is the Mediator of the new covenant, by means of death, for the **redemption of the transgressions** under the first covenant, that those who are called may receive the promise of the eternal inheritance.*

2. Jesus' forgiving seventy times seven "makes an end" or "seals up sin." Jesus' forgiving seventy times seven makes an end of animal "sin offerings."

John 1:29, NKJ
*The next day John saw Jesus coming toward him, and said, **"Behold!** **The Lamb of God who takes away the sin of the world!"***

Hebrews 10:10, NKJ
*By that will we have been sanctified **through the offering of the body of Jesus Christ once for all.***

3. Jesus' forgiveness reconciled ("covered") our "perversity."

Colossians 1:20, KJV
*And, having made peace **through the blood of his cross,** by him to **reconcile** all things unto himself; by him, I say, whether they be things in earth, or things in heaven.*

Romans 5:11, NKJ
*And not only so, but we also rejoice in God **through our Lord Jesus Christ,** through whom we have now received the **reconciliation.***

4. Jesus' forgiving seventy times seven will cause everlasting righteousness to be brought into one's life.

1 Corinthians 1:30, NKJ
*But of Him you are in **Christ Jesus, who became for us** ... **righteousness** and sanctification and redemption.*

Philippians 3:9, NKJ
*And be found in Him, not having my own righteousness, which is from the law, **but that which is through faith (lit., trust) in Christ, the righteousness which is from God by faith (lit., trust)***

5. Jesus' forgiving seventy times seven will seal the Vision of Jesus in us, contrary to all the other erroneous man-made visions of today; and His forgiveness will also seal "the prophet" (Jesus) or "the prophecy" (the witness of Jesus) in us.

Habakkuk 2:3-4, NKJ
³*For **the vision** is yet for an appointed time; But at the end **it (lit., he)** will speak, and it (lit., he) will not lie. Though **it (lit., he)** tarries, wait for it; Because **it (lit., he)** will surely come, **It (lit., he)** will not tarry.* ⁴*"Behold the proud, His soul is not upright in him; But the just shall live by his faith."*

Hebrews 10:37-38, NKJ
³⁷*"For yet a little while, And He who is coming will come and will not tarry.* ³⁸*Now the just shall live by faith; But if anyone draws back, my soul has no pleasure in him."*

Revelation 19:10, NKJ
*… For the testimony of Jesus is **the spirit of prophecy (lit., the spirit of the prophecy).***

6. **Jesus' forgiving seventy times seven is part of the work of the anointing of Christ, Jesus. We have the unction (Jesus' anointing) in us!**

Matthew 16:15-16, NKJ
¹⁵*He said to them, "But who do you say that I am?"* ¹⁶*Simon Peter answered and said, "You are the **Christ (or Anointed One)**, the Son of the living God."*

1 John 2:20, NKJ
*But you have an **anointing** from the Holy One, and you know all things.*

Thus, we have just briefly comprehended how our heavenly Father by our Lord Jesus Christ and through the Spirit of Jesus will make an end of sins through His forgiveness. May the Lord be thanked, praised, and glorified both now and into the ages.

490 Forgiveness in Every Measure

Ezekiel 40:5, NKJ
*... In the **man's** hand was a measuring rod six cubits long, each being a cubit and a handbreadth....*

Psalm 39:5, NKJ
*Indeed, You have made **my days as handbreadths**....*

2 Samuel 5:4, NKJ
*David was **thirty years** old when he began to reign, and he **reigned forty years.***

I believe the Man that appeared to Ezekiel was Jesus. Jesus appeared to Ezekiel with a measuring reed in His hand. This is understood by the description given about this "Man," and the truth that all that is written in the Bible "testifies" about Jesus. This same Jesus is appearing to us in the Spirit with His measuring reed; and He is measuring us. In His measure he is looking for forgiveness.

The Man's measuring reed in Ezekiel 40:5 was made of six cubits. Each cubit in this reed was made of **"a cubit and a handbreadth,"** which is known as the **"great cubit."** Each regular cubit consists of six (6) handbreadths; however, a "great cubit" consists of seven (7) handbreadths. Thus, six (6) handbreadths in the normal cubit, plus the one (1) additional handbreadth makes seven (7) handbreadths in a "great cubit."

For clarity, let us look at a US unit of measure. Let us look at the "reed" as to a "yard stick." There are three (3) feet in one (1) yard; just as there are six (6) cubits in one (1) reed. There are twelve (12) inches in one (1) foot; just as there are seven (7) handbreadths in one (1) "great cubit." We can do the same for the metric unit of measure.

There are one hundred (100) centimeters in one (1) meter; just as there are six (6) cubits in a reed. There are ten (10) millimeters to one (1) centimeter; as there are seven (7) handbreadths to one (1) "great cubit."

With that understood, unit of measure described in Ezekiel's book has prophetic overtones with respect to the four hundred-ninety forgiveness spoken by Jesus. Especially since the Man used seven (7) handbreadths per cubit to define His reed. We will discover that there is forgiveness in every reed that Jesus uses to measure us. This is seen through David's life span.

David in Psalm 39:5 said that his **"days"** are as a **"handbreadth."** David was **thirty (30)** years old when he became king, according to 2 Samuel 5:4-5; and he reigned for **forty (40)** years. This makes David's years that he lived a total seventy (70) years. Therefore, each handbreadth in the "Man's" reed can be equated to "70" years.

Since, there are seven (7) handbreadths in each cubit; "seven handbreadths" equal "seven seventy" (7 times 70) based on the "handbreadth" of "[David's] days." Seven times seventy equals four hundred-ninety (7x70=490), the same number Jesus equates to the "number" related to forgiveness.

The "Man's" reed in Ezekiel's vision consisted of six (6) [great] cubits, with each of the great cubits being a cubit (six handbreadths) and an additional handbreadth. These seven handbreadths also equal "seven-seventy" (again, 70x 70=490 is the number that symbolizes forgiveness).

"Six" (6) is the number that symbolizes man, or mankind. Adam (mankind) was created on the sixth (6th) day. John, the beloved said we can make sense of the number of the beast, "**'because'** it is the **number 'of man'** and his number is 'six hundred sixty-six

(666). Again, six (6) is the number for man and because of sinful man. Thus, in the reed held by the Man (Jesus) is **six, four hundred-ninety.** This means that Jesus has forgiveness (showed by the number "490") for **mankind** (showed by the number "6"). This is awesome. Let us look at this now as the measure of forgiveness relates to us.

Whenever Jesus comes to us to measure our lives, He is looking to see if we have forgiven our fellow brother (man) four hundred-ninety times. When he puts the reed against us in our hearts, will He find the same measure He puts in us, the forgiving of others as He has forgiven us? Looking at it from another perspective, whenever, Jesus measures us there is always forgiveness in His measure.

His measure consists of four hundred-ninety forgiveness for His people and for mankind who turn to Jesus. In every measure of Ezekiel's Temple (symbolic of the "temple of our bodies"); or Ezekiel's New Jerusalem (symbolic of the Church as a city); or Ezekiel's Israel (symbolic of "the Israel of God" — the Church as a holy nation); there is forgiveness for His people.

Whenever Jesus measures us, it is not unto condemnation. Whenever He measures us, He looks for ways to forgive us. In all the measure (12,000 stadia) of New Jerusalem, His Bride, there is forgiveness *(Revelation 21:16)*. In the measure of the wall of the city, the one hundred and forty-four cubits (144 cubits), there is forgiveness for the perfected corporate man *(Revelation 21:17)*. In the measure of 1600 stadia in Revelation 14:20, there is forgiveness unto "obedience."

Finally, as Jesus measures our life, there is "490" forgiveness for us! The Lord loves you and me, enough to forgive you and me of any sins and lawlessness!

The Bosom of 490 Forgiveness

Ezekiel 43:13, NKJ
*These are the measurements of the altar in cubits (**the cubit is one cubit and a handbreadth**): the base (**lit., bosom**) one cubit high and one cubit wide, with a rim all around its edge of one span....*

The "bosom" of the altar ("the place of sacrifice") is also a place of four hundred-ninety forgiveness. As we discovered in the previous chapter, Ezekiel used the "great cubit" as the unit of measure. The great cubit is just a little larger than the normal cubit.

The great "cubit is a cubit and a handbreadth." This "great cubit" is also used for the measurement of the "base" of the altar. The word **"base"** is a Hebrew word that means **"bosom;"** and is translated as such in the Bible.

Ruth 4:16, NKJ
*Then Naomi took the child and laid him on her **bosom and** became a nurse to him.*

The measure of the altar's bosom was "a cubit" after the great cubit consisting of "a cubit and a handbreadth." In the previous chapter, we demonstrated that the "handbreadth" equals seventy years. There are seven handbreadths in a great cubit. Thus, seventy times seven equals four hundred-ninety.

The "altar" is defined as "a place of sacrifice." Jesus' sacrifice is our place of sacrifice. *(Hebrews 9:26).* Jesus is our living Altar *(Hebrews 13:10-12).* As the altar that Ezekiel measured had a bosom, so likewise, our Lord Jesus Christ has a bosom *(John 13:23).* In the bosom of our Lord Jesus, our living Altar, are also four hundred-ninety forgiveness. We can rest our head in the bosom of Jesus as we hear Him say, "You are forgiven!" This is wonderful to know!

As we lay in the bosom of Jesus, our living Altar, we will find answers concerning the truth of forgiveness and the grace of forgiveness. In the bosom of the Father there is grace and truth *(John 1:17-18)*. Jesus said that He does what He sees His Father do *(John 5:19)*.

Therefore, Jesus declares, and does what He has seen in the bosom of the Father. Jesus declares to us the Father's grace, forgiveness, mercy, and the Father's "truth" (the truth of God's four hundred-ninety forgiveness in one day, and so on).

May we all rest our heads (minds) in the bosom of Jesus that we may continue to be comforted by His forgiveness! He always believes we are sincere whenever we ask for forgiveness — "love believes all things;" and He is just to forgive us four hundred-ninety times in one day, as we ask Him for forgiveness; and He is just to forgive as we forgive from our bosoms (hearts), others who may have offended us.

How Often do we Forgive?

Matthew 18:21, NKJ
*Then Peter came to Him and said, "Lord, **how often shall my brother*** *sin against me, and I forgive him? Up to seven times?"*

Jesus gave the Church a process to deal with repetitive sins. No person is to continue to sin because they know that the Father's grace is there for them. "What shall we say then? **Shall we continue in sin,** that grace may abound? **Certainly not! (lit., may it never be birth).** How shall we who died to sin live any longer in it" *(Romans 6:1-2, NKJ)?*

Let us not abuse the forgiveness of our Lord. Continual sinning has limits. The picture of the Mercy Seat (the place of obtaining mercy), also shows that for a season there will be an "end of mercy." Let us not abuse our Lord's grace, or abuse others by continually sinning against them! So, how often do we forgive?

There are many disciples and unbelievers who ask this question today. Peter also asked the same question to the Lord Himself. How long do I keep forgiving my brother if he keeps offending me? Well Jesus gave a procedure for this also.

Step 1:
If someone keeps sinning against you, Jesus said first go to that person in private. "If your brother sins against you, go and show him his fault, **just between the two of you.** If he listens to you, you have won your brother over" *(Matthew 18:15, NIV).* This is the first thing we must do when someone repetitively sins against us. We must first discuss the issue in private. However, most in the Church of today is opposite. They tell the world if someone offends them before they discuss it in private with the offender. Let us do what Jesus said, "go [to your brother/sister] and show

him his fault just between the two of you. If he listens to you, you have won your brother over."

Step 2:
If a private conversation with your offender does not work, then take two others along with you to discuss your offense. But if the offender "will not listen, **take one or two others along,** so that 'every matter may be established by the testimony of two or three witnesses'" *(Matthew 18:16, NIV).* Again, taking an offense beyond a private conversation is done only if private reconciliation did not work.

Step 3:
If a private attempt to reconcile and an attempt to bring reconciliation with two other witnesses do not work, then the matter is to be brought before the Church (not the world). "If he refuses to listen to them, **tell it to the church"** *(Matthew 18:17a, NIV).* This is straightforward enough; if an offender refuses to listen to the complaint of the offended, tell the whole matter to the Church. Going public to the Church is the last resort. It is not the first resort.

This is one of the reasons why there are so many unsolved offenses in the Church today. People take their offenses to the public domain of the Church first; rather that handling matters in private first. If an attempt to reconcile in private does not work; then, and only then, should a person make an offense public to two witnesses; and if the reconciliation with the two witnesses does not work, then take the offense to the Church as a last resort.

Step 4:
If a person that offends another person does not listen to his brother or sister in private and he or she does not listen to the advice of two or three witnesses, and that same person will not even listen to the Church, then the Church can excommunicate

that person. The person is to be treated as a "pagan" and a "tax collector." Matthew said, "If he refuses to listen to them, tell it to the church; and if he refuses to listen even to the church, treat him as you would a pagan or a tax collector" *(Matthew 18:17, NIV).* In the words of Luke, sometimes the qualification for being forgiven of a fault is that the offender must <u>first</u> "repent" of his offences once the offender is enlightened of his or her sin against someone *(Luke 17:3-4).*

By the way, the so called "law of binding and loosing" was used in context of the Church binding a person from fellowshipping with the Church if that person refuses to reconcile with a person that he or she offended, and then refuses to hear the Church's call to reconcile. Listen to the verses again: "If he refuses to listen to them, tell it to the church; and if he refuses to listen even to the church, **treat him as you would a pagan or a tax collector. I tell you the truth, whatever you bind on earth will be bound in heaven,** and whatever you loose on earth will be loosed in heaven" *(Matthew 18:17-18, NIV).*

With all of the above said, we should not be too quick to excommunicate. In context of Jesus' process for excommunication, He also said that we are to forgive our offenders 490 times.

Matthew 18:21-22, NKJ
21Then Peter came to Him and said, "Lord, how often shall my brother sin against me, and I forgive him? Up to seven times?" *22**Jesus said to him, "I do not say to you, up to seven times, but up to seventy times seven."***

Forgiven Ten Thousand Times

Matthew 18:21-23, NKJ
*²¹Then Peter came to Him and said, **"Lord, how often shall my brother sin against me, and I forgive him? Up to seven times?"** ²²Jesus said to him, "I do not say to you, up to seven times, but up to seventy times seven." ²³"Therefore the kingdom of heaven is like a certain king who wanted to settle accounts with his servants. ²⁴And when he had begun to settle accounts, one was brought to him who owed him ten thousand talents."*

Jesus had given a discourse on how to handle folks who keep sinning against one another. Peter then asked our Lord Jesus; how often do we forgive our offenders who keep sinning against us? He responded with an allegory. He likens the kingdom of heaven to an account related to forgiveness.

In this parable Jesus provided some powerful truths. We learn that even though we have myriads of sins; our Master will forgive our debts. However, He also requires that the same way as He forgives our myriads of debts to Him, we must also forgive our fellow man who may owe us just hundreds of pennies.

The parable also teaches us that if we refuse to forgive a person, it is like taking that person by the throat and choking him or her. Jesus' simile also teaches us that if we choose not to forgive, after we have been forgiven; it is like throwing that person into prison. This same parable also teaches that the person, who throws another into the prison of un-forgiveness, will also himself be placed in prison by our heavenly Father.

These points taught us by Jesus encourage us to forgive 490 times. Every human, whether they acknowledge it or not, like to be forgiven by our heavenly Father. We also want the Father to forgive us instantaneously, and we also want Him to forget our sins. If we so expect our heavenly Father to forgive us with no debt left over, He expects us to do the same for mankind. We are forgiven 490 times by our heavenly Father. We ought to forgive our brothers and sisters 490 times from our hearts!

Matthew 18:21-35, NKJ

*21Then Peter came to Him and said, "Lord, how often shall my brother sin against me, and I forgive him? Up to seven times?" 22Jesus said to him, "I do not say to you, up to seven times, but up to seventy times seven. 23"Therefore the kingdom of heaven is like a certain king who wanted to settle accounts with his servants. 24"And when he had begun to settle accounts, one was brought to him who owed him **ten thousand talents (lit., myriads of weights).** 25"But as he was not able to pay, his master commanded that he be sold, with his wife and children and all that he had, and that payment be made. 26"The servant therefore fell down before him, saying, 'Master, have patience with me, and I will pay you all.' 27"Then the master of that servant was moved with compassion, released him, and forgave him the debt. 28"But that servant went out and found one of his fellow servants who owed him a hundred denarii; and he laid hands on him and took him by the throat, saying, 'Pay me what you owe!' 29 "So his fellow servant fell down at his feet and begged him, saying, 'Have patience with me, and I will pay you all.' 30 "And he would not, but went and threw him into prison till he should pay the debt. 31"So when his fellow servants saw what had been done, they were very grieved, and came and told their master all that had been done. 32"Then his master, after he had called him, said to him, 'You wicked servant! I forgave you all that debt because you begged me. 33 'Should you not also have had compassion on your fellow servant, just as I had pity on you?' 34"And his master was angry and delivered him to the torturers until he should pay all that was due to him. 35"So My heavenly Father also will do to you if each of you, from his heart, does not forgive his brother his trespasses."*

We see in the texts above:
1. Debts (sins) are heavy (talents means "weights").
2. Debts <u>have</u> to be repaid <u>or</u> forgiven.

3. Debts affect one's immediate family and possession.
4. Worship appeals to God's patience to repay debts.
5. Worship invokes compassion to release and forgive.
6. Compassion free families from debts (sins).
7. Compassion loose one's property from repossession.
8. Compassion forgives debts.
9. The Father forgives us of "myriads" of debts (sins).
10. Forgive others of their small debts/sins.
11. Un-forgiveness causes physical harm.
12. The attitude of un-forgiveness chokes.
13. Un-forgiveness is not patient with others.
14. Un-forgiveness is a prison.
15. Un-forgiveness is seen by others who then tell God.
16. Un-forgiveness of others reverses one's forgiveness.
17. Un-forgiveness causes the un-forgiver torments.
18. We are to forgive others as the Father has forgiven us.

May we forgive 490 times as the Father through Jesus Christ has forgiven us 10,000 times!

No More Consciousness of Sins

Hebrews 10:1-2, NKJ
*¹For the law, having a shadow of the good things to come, and not the very image of the things, can never with these same sacrifices, which they offer continually year by year, make those who approach perfect. ²For then would they not have ceased to be offered? For the worshipers, once purified, would have had **no more consciousness of sins.***

Hebrews 10:22, NKJ
*Let us draw near with a true heart in full assurance of faith, having our hearts sprinkled from an **evil conscience (lit., a consciousness of evil)** and our bodies washed with pure water.*

Jesus' blood benefits us by sprinkling our hearts from being conscious of evil and sins. We were so trained to always think of how bad things are that Jesus came along to change that consciousness of sins, evil, offences, etc. Believe it, Jesus' sprinkled blood on our conscience is so powerful, it makes us focus on His goodness and not our badness, or the badness of others. We can get to a place in Jesus where we are no longer conscious of our sins. His blood is that strong to purge our conscience.

Hebrews 9:13-14, NKJ
*¹³For if the blood of bulls and goats and the ashes of a heifer, sprinkling the unclean, sanctifies for the purifying of the flesh, ¹⁴how much more shall **the blood of Christ,** who through the eternal Spirit offered Himself without spot to God, **cleanse your conscience from dead works to serve the living God?***

The word for **cleanse** is from the same word family used by Jesus in John 15 that is translated as **prune.** Thus, the blood of Jesus, through the eternal Spirit is able to **prune** or **cut away** dead works (the dead works of not serving God in prayer and fasting because of being overly conscious of one's badness). We must know that once the blood of Jesus is sprinkled in our hearts by faith, that same blood also purges, or cleanse us to be able to serve the living God with prayer and fasting.

Through the blood of Jesus and baptism in the name of Jesus, we can live before God with a good conscience *(Acts 23:1; 1 Peter 3:21)*. Through the blood of Jesus, we can live with a conscience void of striking at people with our thoughts *(Acts 24:16)*. Through the blood of Jesus, we can hold the mystery of the faith in a pure conscience *(1 Timothy 3:9)*. Through the blood of Jesus, we can have an **"ideal"** conscience *(Hebrews 13:18)*. Through the blood of Jesus, we can have a conscience that is conscious of God *(1 Peter 2:19)*.

The conscience is a witness *(Romans 2:15; 9:1; 2 Corinthians 1:12);* **and** the Father wants our conscience to be a good witness in us, presently and in the Day of Judgment. Thus, He has made a provision; He has sprinkled our conscience with the blood of Jesus. Jesus' blood has done what animal sacrifice could not do; Jesus' blood has taken away the consciousness of sins *(Hebrews 9:9; 10:2)*.

We do not have to be conscious of the offenses of others, our past mistakes, or our sins. We will not be judged for the sins that Jesus has forgiven us for. Jesus Himself said that "God sent **not** the Son into the world to judge the world; but that the world should be **saved** through him. **He that believeth on him is not judged:** he that believeth not hath been judged already, because he hath not believed on the name of the only begotten Son of God" *(John 3:17-18, ASV)*. This is good news!

We who believe in the Son (Jesus) are not judged! Here is some more good news; the Father does not remember our sins after He forgives us through Jesus' sacrifice. "Their sins and their lawless deeds I will remember **no more**" *(Hebrews 10:17, NKJ).*

Ezekiel 18:21-23, NKJ
[21]*"But if a wicked man turns from all his sins which he has committed, keeps all My statutes, and does what is lawful and right, he shall surely live; he shall not die.* [22]*"**None of the transgressions** which he has committed shall be **remembered against him;** because of the righteousness which he has done, he shall live.* [23]*"Do I have any pleasure at all that the wicked should die?" says the Lord GOD, "and not that he should turn from his ways and live?*

Because Jesus said we are not judged for believing in Him; and the New Covenant also states that the Father does not remember our sins which we confess to Him asking for His forgiveness; then we are not supposed to be conscious of our badness once we are forgiven, or the offences of others against us once we forgive them; However, we should be conscious of Jesus' forgiveness, and His righteousness imparted to us.

We are to be "God conscious," not revenge conscious, self conscious, fear conscious, and so on *(1 Thessalonians 5:15; 1 Peter 2:19; Genesis 3:10).* Arise and "shake yourself from the dust" of the "down-judging" of the first Adam and be made alive in the forgiveness of the Last Adam, Jesus Christ *(Isaiah 52:2; Genesis 3:19; 1 Corinthians 15:45).*

The Examples of Forgiveness

Luke 23:33-34, NKJ
[33]*And when they had come to the place called Calvary, there they crucified Him, and the criminals, one on the right hand and the other on the left.* [34]*Then Jesus said,* **"Father, forgive them,** *for* **they do not know** *what they do." And they divided His garments and cast lots.*

Jesus is the greatest example of forgiving our offenders. This Man — Jesus — was just sent to His crucifixion by some of the very people who claimed to have followed Him, and by some of His haters (the Pharisees, and teachers of the law).

He was crucified by the hands of the "beast" of that day — the Roman Empire (Daniel's 4th Beast). Jesus was also crucified and categorized with "evil-workers." In the midst of all this injustice to our Messiah, He forgave those who abused Him! This is strong!

Jesus' forgiveness was so effective that some from the same Pharisees sect that killed Him became obedient to the Faith *(Acts 6:7; Acts 15:5)*. Believe it or not, those who murder can be forgiven like the Pharisees who killed Jesus were forgiven. Lamech, a son of Cain, was among the first to use the principle of "490 forgiveness" as a stay of vengeance for an apparent slaying. "Lamech said ... I have killed a man for wounding me, even a young man for hurting me. If Cain shall be avenged sevenfold, then Lamech **seventy-sevenfold**" *(Genesis 4:23-24)*.

Lamech like his father, Cain slew a man. God protected his father Cain from vengeance "sevenfold" *(Genesis 4:15)*. However, Lamech wanted protection from vengeance for slaying a young man 490 times, the "number" that represents forgiveness. Now, I am not advocating justification for killing *(1 Peter 4:15; 1 John 3:15)*. But what I am saying is that genuine repentance to the Lord can bring forgiveness of sins. The great Moses and Paul killed, and the Lord forgave them after they genuinely repented. This is also true for those who commit abortions. Jesus will forgive! Just ask Him for forgiveness!

Jesus exemplifies forgiveness even to those who slay you for no just cause. Like Jesus, if you are being crucified, forgive the abusers! When you are hated for no reason, forgive! When you are numbered as a transgressor, forgive your offenders!

It is Jesus-like to forgive, even in the midst of death. In fact, when one can forgive their killers, Jesus stands up. Yes, one of the accounts that declared Jesus standing up from His throne is when Stephen, before he fell asleep, forgave those who stoned Him to death. What a powerful witness of forgiveness to those who were stoning him.

Yes, this forgiveness by Stephen affected the great apostle Paul, who consented to Stephen's death. Stephen's forgiveness so affected Paul, that Paul reminded Jesus of his involvement in Stephen's death in a conversation with the Lord *(Acts 22:20)*. With that said, here is the account of Jesus standing for Stephen.

Acts 7:55-60, NKJ
*55But he, being full of the Holy Spirit, gazed into heaven and saw the glory of God, and **Jesus standing at the right hand of God,** 56and said, "Look! **I see** the heavens opened and the Son of Man **standing** at the right hand of God!" 57 Then they cried out with a loud voice, stopped their ears, and ran at him with one accord; 58and they cast him out of the city and stoned him. And the witnesses laid down their clothes at the feet of a young man named Saul. 59And **they stoned Stephen** as he was calling on God and saying, "Lord Jesus, receive my spirit." 60 **Then he knelt down and cried out with a loud voice, "Lord, do not charge them with this sin."** And when he had said this, he fell asleep.*

Stephen saw the Lord "Jesus standing" on his behalf as Stephen witnessed to the Jews who eventually stoned him to death after he finished his testimony of Jesus. The Lord honors those who testify of Him; and He honors those who can forgive even those who killed the Saints just for testifying of the truth. The apostle Paul also demonstrated something similar.

2 Timothy 4:16, NIV
*At my first defense, no one came to my support, but everyone deserted me. **May it not be held against them.***

At Paul's first defense with respect to his imprisonment at Rome, He said, "No one came to my support, but **everyone** deserted me." In this case the merciful apostle made a plea. He forgave them by saying, **"May it not be held against them!"** We ought to do the same. When we are forsaken, forgive! When men do not stand with you as expected, forgive them!

Jesus is our pattern. He forgives! We must also forgive! He forgave those who slew Him! We must also forgive! What a loving heart Jesus has! In the pain of being slain, Jesus forgave. Brothers and sisters, I conclude this chapter with this message; **"Be kind and compassionate to one another, forgiving each other, just as in Christ God forgave you"** *(Ephesians 4:32).*

There is no Condemnation!

Romans 8:1; 9a, NKJV
*¹There is therefore now **no condemnation** to **those who are in Christ Jesus,** who do not walk according to the flesh, but according to the Spirit... ⁹But you are not in the flesh but in the Spirit, if indeed the Spirit of God dwells in you....*

"In Christ Jesus" is a special place. "In Christ Jesus," there is no condemnation. What a relief! All the Church and the world needs to know this experientially. "Condemnation" means "down-judging." There is no "down-judging" to those in Christ Jesus! (I am fully aware that I am being repetitive! I want this truth to sink in.) Most of us "cut our teeth" on the ministry of condemnation. Let me explain!

Some get saved, and some hear messages of condemnation! Some have grown up from their youth under condemnation. Some even condemn themselves. However, "in Christ Jesus" there is **"now"** no condemnation to those who have Christ's Spirit. Let me say that again, **"now"** — presently — there is no condemnation to you if you are in Christ Jesus.

"In Christ" means that you believe in the Lord Jesus Christ and you should also be baptized in water in Jesus' name; and you should also be "in the Spirit" by being filled with the Spirit of Jesus. "You are not in the flesh but in the Spirit, if indeed the Spirit of God dwells in you" **(Romans 8:9a).**

John 3:18, ASV
He that believeth on him is not judged: *he that believeth not hath been judged already, because he hath not believed on the name of the only begotten Son of God.*

Jesus Himself said it, "He that believes on Him (Jesus) is not judged." What a relief. **"Who shall lay anything to the charge of God's elect? It is God** that justifies. Who is he that condemns" *(Romans 8:33-34a)?*

How can preachers continue to condemn others? They did not die for anyone's sins like Jesus did. "It is Christ Jesus that died, yea rather, that was raised from the dead, who is at the right hand of God, **who also makes intercession for us"** *(see Romans 8:34).*

Romans 8:31-39, NKJ
[31]What then shall we say to these things? ***If God is for us, who can be against us?*** *[32] He who did not spare His own Son, but delivered Him up for us all, how shall He not with Him also freely give us all things?* *[33]* ***Who shall bring a charge against God's elect? It is God who justifies.*** *[34]* ***Who is he who condemns?*** *It is Christ who died, and furthermore is also risen, who is even at the right hand of God, who also makes intercession for us.* *[35]****Who shall separate us from the love of Christ?*** *Shall tribulation, or distress, or persecution, or famine, or nakedness, or peril, or sword?* *[36]As it is written: "For Your sake we are killed all day long; We are accounted as sheep for the slaughter."* *[37]Yet in all these things we are more than conquerors through Him who loved us.* *[38]****For I am persuaded*** *that neither death nor life, nor angels nor principalities nor powers, nor things present nor things to come,* *[39]nor height nor depth, nor any other created thing,* ***shall be able to separate us from the love of God which is in Christ Jesus our Lord.***

Stop condemning yourself, and do not allow others to condemn you. God already knows those who love Him (that is, those who love the Father, because He first loved us). For those who love God, all things (all inclusive) will work together for good (theirs and others). God predestined those who love Him to be conformed to the image of Jesus. Here is the process:

1. Those He predestined, He also called them.

2. Those whom He called, He justified.
3. Those whom He justifies, He will glorify them.

Romans 8:29-30, NIV

[29]For those God foreknew he also predestined to be conformed to the likeness of his Son, that he might be the firstborn among many brothers. [30]And **those he predestined, he also called; those he called, he also justified; those he justified, he also glorified.**

Herein is the part that appears to take the Father the longest, the Father's work to bring us to that "pre-place"[3] as "son of glory." It is difficult for the Father to glorify[4] us in the earth until He convinces us that we are indeed justified.[5] We are not condemned! We are justified; and the Father will take a lifetime if necessary, to convince us that we are indeed justified! There is "now" no condemnation to those who are in Christ Jesus!

You are predestined to be conformed to Jesus' image. Therefore, the Father called you for that purpose. This is your calling, to be like Jesus, to be a "placed mature son" in the kingdom of God. The Father justified you by raising Jesus from the dead, who is now interceding for all of us! Eventually, glory to God, we will be glorified both in the Father's work and in resurrection by the Father, through Jesus.

In Christ Jesus, you are not cursed, you are not condemned, and you are not judged! YOU ARE FORGIVEN 490! Amen!

---

[3] In Gal 4:2, "time appointed" is literally "preplaced." We are preplaced to "son-ship."
[4] 1 Cor 2:7-10; Heb 2:10; Rom 8:18; John 2:11 w/John 2:1-10
[5] An understanding the Lord gave Judith (my wife) a few years ago.

Other Books

- Poiema, by Judith Peart
- Wisdom from Above, by Judith Peart
- Procreation, Understanding Sex and Identity by Judith Peart
- 100 Nevers, by Judith Peart
- The Shattered and the Healing by Judith Peart
- The Lamb, by Donald Peart
- Jesus' Resurrection, Our Inheritance, by Donald Peart.
- Sexuality, By Donald Peart
- Forgiven 490, by Donald Peart w/Judith Peart!
- The Days of the Seventh Angel, By Donald Peart
- The Torah (The Principle) of Giving, by Donald Peart
- The Time Came, by Donald Peart
- The Last Hour, the First Hour, the Forty-Second Generation, by Donald Peart
- Vision Real, by Donald Peart
- The False Prophet, Alias, Another Beast V1, by Donald Peart
- Son of Man Prophesy Against the false prophet, by Donald Peart
- The Many False Prophets (The Dragon's Tail), by Donald Peart
- The Work of Lawlessness Revealed, by Donald Peart
- When the Lord Made the Tempter, by Donald Peart
- Examining Doctrine, Volume 1, by Donald Peart
- Exousia, Your God Given Authority, by Donald Peart
- The Numbers of God, by Donald Peart
- The Completions of the Ages, the Gate, the Door, and the Veil, by Donald Peart
- The Revelation of Jesus Christ, by Donald Peart
- Jude –Translation-Commentary, by Donald Peart
- The Better Resurrection, the Person, the Event, and the Age, by Donald Peart
- Manifestations from Our Lord Jesus Christ by Donald and Judith Peart
- You Exist! (Understanding Your Identity) by Donald Peart
- The New Testament Dr. Donald Peart Exegesis
- The Tree of Life, By Dr. Donald Peart
- The Spirit and Power of John, the Baptist by Dr. Donald Peart
- Is She Married to a Husband? by Donald Peart
- The Ugliest Man God Made by Donald Peart
- Does Answering the Call of God Impact Your Children? by Donald Peart
- Victory Out-of-the Beast-the Harvest of the Earth by Donald Peart
- Melchizedek by Donald Peart
- Ezekiel-the House-the City-the Land (Interpreting the Patterns) by Donald Peart
- Butter & Honey, Understanding How to Choose the Good and Refuse Evil, by Donald Peart

Contact Information:

Crown of Glory Ministries
P.O. Box 1041 Randallstown, MD 21133
donaldpeart7@gmail.com

About the Author:
Donald Peart is married to Judith Peart since 1986; and they believe that Jesus is the Christ, the Son of the living God; and they teach the gospel of God's kingdom centered on Jesus Christ and His ecclesia. They are the parents of six children, including their daughter-in-law. They have founded and currently oversee Crown of Glory Ministries in Randallstown, Maryland. Donald and his wife have written over thirty-six books; and their ministry has distributed their book to at least 29 States in the USA and 21 countries. In his early years of ministry, the Lord Jesus graced Donald to have studied the Word of God extensively and in depth (sometimes studying for over 8 hours per day for many years). The Lord Jesus has graced Donald to earn an Associate of Arts degree in Pre-Engineering, a Bachelor of Science degree in Civil Engineering, a Master of Divinity, a Master of Science in Construction Management, and a Doctorate in Theology.